ORVILLE REDENBACHER'S
Popcorn Book

ORVILLE REDENBACHER'S
Popcorn Book

BY ORVILLE REDENBACHER

ST. MARTIN'S PRESS   NEW YORK

10 9 8 7 6 5 4 3 2 1

I dedicate this book to the memory of my parents—without whom there wouldn't be an Orville Redenbacher; to my partners and good friends, Charlie Bowman and Carl Hartman, without whom there wouldn't be an Orville Redenbacher's® Gourmet® Popping Corn; to my lovely wife, Nina, without whom I wouldn't care to be; and to the fourth generation, which has just started, T. Grant Gourley.

☞ CONTENTS ☜

☞ FOREWORD ☜

Hello. I'm Orville Redenbacher and first of all, I want to make it clear that I am real. Now, a lot of folks don't believe that for some reason. They seem to think I'm an actor hired to play the part of The Popcorn King. Well, while it's true that I do have more than a little ham in me, the rest is popcorn. I've crusaded most of my life to do away with unspeakably ordinary popcorn and replace it with a Gourmet® Popping Corn that pops up virtually 100 percent and is lighter, fluffier, and better tasting. I succeeded, and now I'm called the King—and if you still don't believe me, just ask anyone in Valparaiso, Indiana, my hometown, whether I'm real or not.

I got involved with popcorn originally because I was dissatisfied with the popcorn available. I wrote this book for the same reason. There's been an awful lot of misinformation circulating about popping corn, so I decided to set the record straight.

This is the complete and concrete Official Guide to Popping Corn and I've left no kernel unturned in my effort to bring you the whole story of a native American food. Popcorn is more than just pure fun and good eating; it's a matter of historical importance and a source of national pride. There are also plenty of good recipes in here.

You have a lot to look forward to, and I hope you enjoy every bit of it.

Sincerely,

Orville Redenbacher

Orville Redenbacher

ORVILLE REDENBACHER'S
Popcorn Book

The Kernel Journal

Some of you may think that popcorn is a pretty newfangled foodstuff, invented to go with the movies. Let me offer you a piece of advice: don't take any bets on it!

Anthropologists found 5,600-year-old popcorn ears in the Bat Caves of New Mexico on the site of an Indian settlement. The ears measured under 2 inches in length, but they were mighty! Incan tombs, more than a thousand years old, were found to hold jewels and gold and precious artifacts—such as popcorn kernels. (The research teams really did their research: the popcorn was still poppable after all those years!)

On his way here, Columbus encountered the natives of the West Indies, including some "street vendors" who were hawking popcorn decorations that looked something like corsages. (I think popcorn is real pretty, too, and if you like the idea of decorating with it, please see the chapters on How to Make Popcorn Blush, and Other Party Tricks, and I Get a Little Corny at Christmas.)

The Aztecs also used popcorn as a decoration, as well as a food, embellishing their ceremonial headdresses, stringing it in necklaces, and ornamenting the statues of their gods. During the popcorn growing season, statues of Tlaloc, the God of Maize, Rain, and Fertility, were wreathed with strands of popcorn.

Fossilized corn pollen, not much different from modern corn pollen, was found in an excavation some 200 feet below Mexico City. And a Zapotec funeral urn, dating back to about A.D. 300, depicts a Maize god both holding and wearing what appears to be popping corn.

Orville Redenbacher with a jar of his Gourmet® Popping Corn.

By the time European settlers arrived in the New World, popcorn and other types of corn had spread to all Indian tribes in both Americas except those farthest north and farthest south, where it just wouldn't grow. The Iroquois were, from all accounts, most adept with popping. They even passed on a recipe for popcorn soup to colonial housewives. It was the Iroquois who introduced the colonists to popping corn, which might have had a lot to do with the fact that the colonists survived those early years and multiplied. The first puffed breakfast cereal eaten by the white man, served up with sugar and cream, was popcorn. After all, it is a whole grain. Popcorn quickly became a staple food that was also much appreciated because it could be stored for a long time without spoiling.

It still is. In 1982, North Americans consumed 9.7 billion quarts of popcorn, or 42 quarts for each man, woman, and child. It remains one of the most wholesome and economical foods available. And, in my opinion, one of the best tasting!

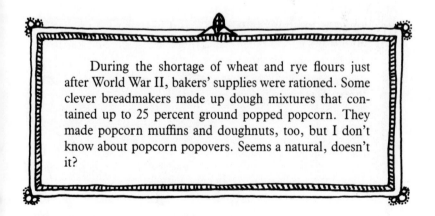

During the shortage of wheat and rye flours just after World War II, bakers' supplies were rationed. Some clever breadmakers made up dough mixtures that contained up to 25 percent ground popped popcorn. They made popcorn muffins and doughnuts, too, but I don't know about popcorn popovers. Seems a natural, doesn't it?

☛ 2 ☚

Meandering Through a Maze of Maize

I'm going to talk about corn for a minute before I tell you about maize, and then about the most amazing maize of all—popcorn.

By rights, popping corn should be called popping maize. The problem is that the word "corn" was used historically for the leading cereal crop of a particular region. In England, corn means wheat, and in Scotland it means oats, and the corn referred to in the Bible was probably barley. When the English got over here and were introduced by the Indians to maize, naturally they just called it corn.

Now, the grain we're talking about here is really maize—even though it's called corn—and there are five basic kinds of it. Of course, each of those has been hybridized and refined and improved, which is how my Gourmet® Popping Corn came about, but let's stick to basics first:

☛ SWEET CORN

Sweet corn is so called because its kernels are sweeter than those of other kinds of corn—it's higher in sugar content. It's also called corn-on-the-cob when you're lucky enough to get it that way, fresh from the stalk and plunged briefly into

4

cooking water. (Nina adds a little bit of milk to bring out the sweetness even more.) The kernels are soft and milky when sweet corn is first picked, and I think it's one of the best eating vegetables there are.

☞ DENT CORN

Dent corn is generally raised for livestock feed, although we also get corn meal, corn flakes, corn oil, and corn syrup from it. An accumulation of soft starches on top of the kernel results in a dent on the crown. It's the most common kind of corn here and in other countries. Europeans, for instance, grow a great deal of dent corn to feed their cattle and other animals, but they don't grow much corn for eating themselves so they can't really understand why sweet corn and popping corn are so popular here. They should try ours.

☞ FLINT CORN

Flint corn looks kind of like flint rock. It's the handsome, multicolored corn you see hung on doors as decorations and used in table centerpieces each fall. It's also called Indian corn. I personally think it would have been more appropriate to honor the Indians by naming sweet corn after them, because if they hadn't introduced the early settlers to it this country might not be settled yet. Still, it's the thought that counts.

☞ POD CORN

Pod corn is the most unusual. The ears are kind of short and squatty, with each and every kernel covered by its own individual husk. Since you could starve while trying to husk enough of it to eat, we dry it instead and use it in flower arrangements, where it has some redeeming value.

☞ POPCORN

This is the real cream of the crop in my book. Popping corn is the more accurate name, and the one I grew up calling it by, but we're an impatient people so the shortened version has stuck. Popcorn is the only corn that pops. You can experiment if you like and dry out some sweet corn to pop, or use what's left of the flint corn from the Thanksgiving cornucopia, but you're going to be disappointed. It won't pop, but it will parch, which means that it will explode partially. You can eat it that way, but it isn't as tasty as popcorn.

Popping corn (old habits die hard) is mostly hard starch, but inside each kernel there is a tiny measure of moisture. If you put popcorn in your popper and get the temperature just right, this droplet of moisture turns to steam and the steam builds up pressure until it finally explodes to many times its original volume.

Some folks prefer white popcorn to yellow popcorn, which is like preferring brown eggs to white eggs, a matter of style rather than taste, although some claim they can tell the difference. (I can't, and I have a highly developed popcorn palate!) Anyway, I grow both, of course, because I want everybody to be happy. Whichever hue you choose, you'll find my brand bred to be superior.

I've read that the Indians thought that popcorn popped because there was a demon living inside each kernel and he got mad when put near heat. The hotter the heat got, the hotter he got, until he just exploded. While anger can do that to you, there's no truth to that particular story. The Indians were wrong about why popcorn pops, but not about its good eating.

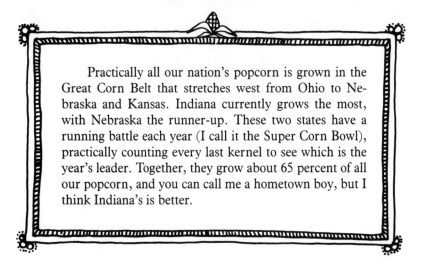

Practically all our nation's popcorn is grown in the Great Corn Belt that stretches west from Ohio to Nebraska and Kansas. Indiana currently grows the most, with Nebraska the runner-up. These two states have a running battle each year (I call it the Super Corn Bowl), practically counting every last kernel to see which is the year's leader. Together, they grow about 65 percent of all our popcorn, and you can call me a hometown boy, but I think Indiana's is better.

☞ HULL, NO!

While it grieves me to say this, some popcorn breeders and packagers actually call their popcorn "hull-less." Well, it just isn't true. There is no such thing as hull-less popcorn and there never will be. Without hulls, there wouldn't even be popcorn.

When the popcorn is bred to have a high popability, as mine is, the result is that the hull explodes harder and shatters into tiny fragments that make it seem as if there was no hull to begin with. That makes the popcorn much more fun to eat, but you can't call it hull-less.

☞ 3 ☜
How to Make a Hybrid

This brings us to All You Ever Wanted to Know About the Sex Life of a Popcorn Plant.

Some say you can't fool Mother Nature; however, if you are going to create a new gourmet popcorn hybrid that is superior to all other popcorns then you have to play with the sex life of a popcorn plant. Since hybridization is not an exact science, the creation of an improved popcorn hybrid requires years and years of hard work plus a few lucky breaks.

For starters, each and every popcorn stalk is bisexual.

The tassel at the top is the male, and it sheds thousands of grains of pollen just like most other flowering plants do. The winds scatter most of this pollen, and the pollen lands on the silks that protrude from the ear shoot on the side of the plant. The silk is the female part of the popcorn plant. Each silk is attached to the individual ovaries on the cob. Only one grain of pollen needs to land anywhere on one of the silks and it will immediately grow down to the ovary and start growing a kernel of popcorn.

To create the pure lines you need to develop a new hybrid, you've got to start with varieties that carry attributes you want to pass on to new generations—higher yield or greater strength or whatever. Years ago, Carl Hartman, our breeding expert, created a synthetic germ plasm by cross-

Orville Redenbacher and Carl Hartman hybridizing popping corn.

pollinating every variety of popcorn he could find. He planted them all together, on one acre, over 30,000 stalks worth, and let the wind and Mother Nature do their stuff.

The result was a hodgepodge—early corn and late corn, short corn and tall corn, fat corn and skinny corn. When the corn reached maturity, he picked those that looked best in terms of desired attributes and bred them back on themselves for ten generations to get pure lines. In 1965 we had our major breakthrough—the highest popping volume ratio in the industry. And it remains a record today.

Here are the steps you have to follow to create pure lines for hybridizing popping corn:

1. Cover the ear shoot with a silk bag before the silks emerge.
2. When the silks start to appear, cover the tassel with a paper bag so you can collect pollen from the same stalk.
3. After the pollen bag has been on for twenty-four hours, shake the tassel before removing the tassel bag to get the greatest amount of pollen. Remove the shoot bag covering the silks quickly, dump the pollen on the exposed silks, and then cover with the bag that has been used to collect the pollen and staple so the wind cannot blow it away.

This is called in-breeding and must be repeated for approximately ten generations. After you have selected two pure lines, you use one for the male and a second one for the female and cross them in the same manner. This creates a single cross hybrid.

As I said before, the hybridization of popcorn is not an exact science, so it requires a lot of patience and a lot of know-how.

☞ 4 ☜

The Proper Popper

☞ **PAST PROPER POPPERS**

Probably the earliest method of popping corn was just to toss it on the glowing coals of a fire and let 'er rip. A lot of popcorn would fall back into the fire, so the technique got more sophisticated with the laying of stones on the fire and the laying of kernels on the stones. Some Indian tribes spread the kernels in hot sand, which at least distributed the heat evenly.

Pottery poppers were around as long as 1,500 years ago, in Mexico and South America. The custom of pot popping traveled, and the Papago tribe in Arizona still pops its corn in large clay vessels—sometimes as big as eight feet across.

With Yankee ingenuity, early colonists fashioned poppers of punched sheet iron, but getting to the popcorn as it popped was still a matter of catch-as-catch-can. They solved the problem by rolling the sheets into cylinders and turning them on axles in front of the fire. These poppers looked kind of like those containers used for the numbers at Bingo games.

You can still find reproductions of these and other types of early metal poppers, and they look real nice hanging next to a fireplace, but they usually don't hold much popcorn and, anyway, modern technology intervened to improve things a great deal.

11

☞ PLAIN OLD POTS AND PANS

The invention of the stove was a big help in itself, and some folks still prefer to pop their popping corn in lidded pots right over the burner, shaking up a storm to keep the kernels moving. You have to keep them in motion because if they just lie around they're liable to burn. A lot of attention—and a lot of agitation—are required.

☞ PLUGGING INTO POPCORN

Less bothersome are the *nonautomatic* electric poppers. When they're plugged in they start building up heat right away, getting hotter and hotter, so you do have to hustle and pour out the popcorn as soon as the popping is completed. Remember to pull the plug too.

Automatic electric poppers have built-in thermostats that bring the heat to the proper popping temperature and keep it there. While they cool down automatically when the temperature starts to get too hot, they don't turn off by themselves so you need to push the switch to Off or unplug the plug when the popping has run its course.

Some poppers are designed with butter dispensers right in the lid. These save you the trouble of melting butter in a separate pan and pouring it over. Unfortunately, they increase the amount of steam inside the popper, which toughens the popcorn.

There are also hot air poppers on the market these days that use no oil at all. I happen to prefer the taste of popcorn popped with hot oil instead of hot air—not only is the flavor better to my way of thinking, but you need the oil to make the salt and other seasonings stick to the popcorn.

There can be other problems with these poppers: either the kernels get pushed away from the heat before they get a chance to pop, or the air temperature is simply not hot enough to pop the corn. The results are not as satisfactory as a real popcorn lover might demand.

Some years ago, after perfecting my Gourmet® Popping Corn, I went on the warpath against imperfect popcorn poppers. Some had heating elements that were too small, bowls that were too flat, no steam vents to allow the steam to escape—and these were all real problems for true popcorn lovers. Anyway, the Popcorn Institute in Chicago started a program of having professional labs test poppers, and we came up with some standards for the industry.

If you're buying a new popper for yourself or as a gift, look for the Popcorn Institute's Seal of Quality Performance, which means that the popper has been tested for ease of operation, safety, and consistent production of high-quality popcorn. The popper has to live up to its advertising and the popcorn it produces has to be crisp and flavorful or the seal is not issued. You'll find the Seal of Quality Performance on the carton or on the directions packed in with the popper, so look for it. For a list of appliances that have earned the seal, write to The Popcorn Institute, 111 East Wacker Drive, Chicago, IL 60601.

☞ 5 ☜
How a Farm Boy from Indiana Grew Up to Be King

It's the darnedest thing. I was always told that any boy could grow up to become President, but I never did aspire to royalty, so you can imagine my surprise when I read in the newspaper one day that I had become America's official Popcorn King. Hard work does pay off!

I was born and reared in Indiana, and my taste for popcorn developed right at home. Dad grew it in our garden, so naturally popcorn was one of our favorite family treats. During grade school and high school, I made my spending money raising popcorn.

My alma mater, Purdue University (from which I was graduated in 1928), pioneered research in popcorn hybridization, back in the 1920s, while I was working for my B.S. in agriculture.

During the years when I taught agriculture and worked as a county agricultural agent in Indiana, I was still especially fascinated with the production of hybrid corn and popcorn seed. I was fascinated with mass communication, too, and became the first county agent to do radio broadcasts from my office and from mobile units. I even went on to do my graduate work in radio communications at Purdue and at Colorado State. I haven't stopped communicating since, or hybridizing, either! In any case, early on I organized and for twelve years

Orville playing the sousaphone as a member of the 1925 ROTC marching band for Purdue University.

managed Princeton Farms, where we grew hybrid popcorn seed and commercial popcorn.

In 1952 Charlie Bowman, my friend since he graduated from Purdue, and I went into business for ourselves, and after a bit Carl Hartman, who is a truly fine professional plant breeder, joined our team. Working together we developed the genuinely superior popping corn I had been searching for since boyhood.

Well, the popcorn industry didn't want it, because my Gourmet® seed and the Gourmet® Popping Corn were both more expensive to produce, because they are both lower in yield per acre than ordinary popcorn. It also cost more to

Orville measuring the popping value of his popping corn in the laboratory.

harvest, to process, and to package. In order to keep up the quality started by the seed, you just had to be consistent and take the extra time, make the extra effort, all along the way. The industry people just figured consumers would say "Popcorn is popcorn" and buy whatever was around. Fooled them, didn't we?

Now, you know my Gourmet® Popping Corn is superior to ordinary popcorn, but maybe you don't know why. I'm going to tell you.

My Gourmet® Popping Corn is the result of forty generations (that's generations of popcorn, not people) of fancy seed hybridization. It's a Snowflake variety of corn that looks kind of like a cumulus cloud when it's popped, and, like snowflakes, each kernel pops up differently. No two are alike. However, once it's popped I'm usually more interested in eating it than eyeing it.

My Gourmet® Popping Corn has a higher popping volume than any of the others; it's bred to. We start with the special seed and we get special popcorn. It's harvested with an ear corn picker instead of a combine, which damages some of the kernels. After drying slowly with warm air on the ear, the corn is shelled with a mechanical sheller. My unique hybrid and its moisture content control are the keys to the corn's popability. By drying it so slowly, we get the exact moisture level ($13\frac{1}{4}$ percent) in each kernel, which creates the nearly 100 percent pop of my popcorn.

About that popping volume: the ordinary popping corn pops less enthusiastically than mine by about 20 percent. Those kernels just don't explode in as spirited a manner as I think is necessary. For good popping corn, you need one with pizzazz. That means that when we do laboratory measurements with our glass tubes, my popping corn pops forty-four times higher than its sitting size. That, in turn, means that it pops harder than others and that it pops up lighter and fluffier and more delicate. As a result, you get more in terms of both quantity and quality. It takes just ½ cup of my special kernels to make a large 4-quart popperful of pure fun and good eating.

Just prior to packaging, the popcorn kernels go through four rigorous tests performed by a cleaner, aspirator, gravity separator, and polisher. All kernels that do not meet the Gourmet® standards of weight and size are tossed out. This ensures that kernels in the filled jar are uniform. And the jar with its screw-top lid was designed to ensure the moisture content control.

It all translates to quality. And it's one of the few items of quality that is still affordable too. Go ahead and hold out for my Gourmet® brand. You deserve it.

And, I've got to admit it, being King isn't half bad.

☞ 6 ☜
Mastering the Art of Pop

Now, I'm no philistine, but I do appreciate the art of pop more than I do pop art. For one thing, you get to eat the results instead of just looking at them, and I'm a man who has his priorities straight.

I've explained all that we do to make my Gourmet® Popping Corn a truly superior corn, and I'd hate to see you ruin it by popping it incorrectly. As with any other kind of cooking, you should start with the finest ingredients and then handle them with respect. In this case, proportion is everything. Here are my rules for getting the biggest bowl of the best-tasting popped corn, every single time.

1. The popper. Many folks today use electric poppers, which do save work and worry. But if you'd rather use a pot, pan, skillet, Dutch oven, or automatic fry pan, go right ahead. Just be sure the bottom is heavy, the lid vents off the steam, and the heat is set at medium. Good popping requires uniform heat. If you pop corn in a wire basket over an open fire (not recommended, though), hold it far enough above the coals or flame so the corn won't scorch!

2. Measure, or man your brooms! Measure out one part oil to three parts popping corn. I prefer my Gourmet®

Courtesy of Thomas S. England, Peoples Weekly, © *1978,* Time, Inc.

Buttery Flavor® Popping Oil. (Never use butter. It will burn.) It is truly important to measure my Gourmet® Popping Corn, because it pops up to forty-four times or more its unpopped volume. (The ordinary popcorns pop up about thirty-four times, so you can see how my care pays off at popping time.) This means that ½ cup of my corn and 3 tablespoons of oil will make a full 4-quart popperful. If you put in too much of my corn, it may lift the lid and start popping all over the room.

3. Cooking the corn. First, put the oil into the popping utensil. Then add popcorn, cover, and heat.

4. Let off steam. If you're using a skillet or pan to pop in, be sure to leave the lid slightly ajar to allow steam to escape during popping.

   As the moisture explodes the corn, it releases steam. If the steam can't escape, it will make the popped corn tough and soggy.

5. Shake. If you're using a skillet or pan, shake the pan to make sure every kernel is heated equally so that none burn or scoot off to the side. When popping slows, remove the pan from heat or unplug the popper.

6. If you're using salt, salt after popping. I strongly recommend using fine-grained popcorn salt rather than regular table salt. You can use less and still get great salt taste. It clings better and won't all land in the bottom of the bowl. Many stores have it, either on the salt shelf or the popcorn shelf.

7. I think my Gourmet® Popping Corn is so good that all you need is a hungry person. But if you'd like the flavor of butter without its high calories, try popping with my Gourmet® Buttery Flavor® Popping Oil instead of popping in oil and then adding butter to the popped corn. If you simply love butter and your

conscience allows . . . melt, pour, and toss with the popped corn in a big bowl.

8. Put the lid back on. My corn comes in screw-top jars to keep it fresh between poppings. Do your part by putting the lid back on nice and tight, and store away from heat. No need to refrigerate as the jar protects the corn from moisture changes. Gourmet® Popping Corn pops larger and fluffier if it is stored at room temperature.

9. Dig in!

Master of Pop Science

I, Orville Redenbacher, take great pleasure in hereby awarding the highest honor in the field of Pop Science to _____, who has studied with fastidious attention and a meticulous eye the finer points of pop, leaving no kernel unattended, no element to chance, in the quest for perfect popcorn poppery.

May the honoree gain much in pop-ularity by sharing this knowledge and this art with the rest of the pop-ulation.

☞ 7 ☜
It Runs in the Family

I'm not saying that I've been a workaholic, but the popcorn profession has taken up a great deal of my time and my energies. With an attitude of "If you can't beat him, join him," most of my family managed to get in on the act. They've all been out in the fields, or the labs, or the offices working at one time or another, but most of them prefer to collaborate in the kitchen.

Here are some of our favorite family recipes.

Orville's Pure Popcorn

Just pop my Gourmet® Popping Corn, shake on popcorn salt to taste, and eat it quickly!

Nina's Favorite Topping

1/4 cup popcorn salt
2 tsp. chili powder
1 tsp. paprika
1 tsp. imitation butter-flavored salt
1/8 tsp. onion powder

Combine flavorings, pour into a shaker, and sprinkle on my freshly popped popcorn at will.

Daughter Sue's Maple Popcorn

4 qts. popped Orville Redenbacher's® Gourmet® Popping Corn
1 cup sugar
2 tbs. water
1/4 tsp. maple flavoring

Keep popcorn warm in 200°F oven in a large, greased pan. Meanwhile, in a heavy saucepan, combine sugar and water over medium heat; stir until clear. Add maple flavoring. Pour syrup over popcorn; stir until all kernels are coated. Return to 200° oven for 20 minutes; stir once or twice. Makes 4 quarts.

My daughter Billie Ann claims that her First Favorite popcorn experience came at her wedding. It was held in the garden, and afterward we all tossed popcorn at the newlyweds instead of rice. She's a little sentimental on the subject, but it did seem appropriate and the birds seemed to enjoy the change in their diets, too.

Daughter Billie Ann's Second Favorite: Parsley Butter Popcorn

4 qts. popped Orville Redenbacher's® Gourmet®
   Popping Corn
½ cup snipped parsley
½ tsp. salt
¼ cup butter, melted
⅛ tsp. garlic powder

In a large bowl, combine popcorn, parsley, and salt. Combine butter and garlic powder; pour over popcorn. Toss until evenly coated. Serve as cocktail appetizer or snack. Makes 4 quarts.

Daughter Gail's Blue Cheese Popcorn Toss

4 qts. popped Orville Redenbacher's® Gourmet®
   Popping Corn
¼ cup butter
1 oz. blue cheese, crumbled
½ tsp. seasoned salt

Put popcorn in large bowl; place in 200°F oven. Meanwhile, in a small saucepan melt butter and blue cheese over low heat; add salt. Pour blue cheese mixture over warm popcorn; toss until all kernels are coated. Serve with soup or salad or as a snack. Makes 4 quarts.

My sister Mabel developed her own family recipe for caramel corn. It's the best I've ever tasted. She often gives it as a hostess gift, packed in canisters she makes from empty food containers with their tight-fitting lids. It's one more reason we just love to have Mabel come visit us!

Orville looks on while his sister Mabel Schafer cooks her recipe for Caramel Corn.

Sister Mabel's Caramel Corn

---

     2 cups light brown sugar, firmly packed
    ½ cup light corn syrup
    ½ lb. margarine or butter
    ¼ tsp. cream of tartar
     1 tsp. salt
     1 tsp. baking soda
     6 qts. popped Orville Redenbacher's® Gourmet®
        Popping Corn (two batches)

In a 2½-quart saucepan combine brown sugar, corn syrup, margarine or butter, cream of tartar, and salt. Bring to a boil, stirring, over medium high heat. Stirring constantly, boil rapidly to hard ball stage, 260°F (about 5 minutes). Remove from heat. Stir in baking soda quickly but thoroughly; pour at once over popcorn in a large roasting or baking pan. Stir gently until all kernels are coated. Bake at 200°F for 1 hour, stirring two or three times during baking. Turn out at once on wax paper; spread apart and allow to cool completely. Break apart; store in a tightly covered container. Makes 6 quarts.

☞ 8 ☜
A Public Service Announcement

People often ask me to what I attribute my success. I always answer the same way: a supportive network of family and friends, curiosity, common sense, stubbornness, tenacity, dreams, and the 4-H. Maybe especially the 4-H. I started in 4-H as a skinny 11-year-old kid with a 4-H Club pig, and I've stuck with them (and they've stuck with me) ever since. 4-H stands for "Head, Heart, Hands, and Health." 4-H is about building better citizens, teaching values, and developing the skills necessary to leading a good (and profitable) life—and it doesn't matter if you're from a farm environment or from a big city. 4-H worked for me, and I've continued to work for it on both local and national levels, organizing the first Junior 4-H Leadership Club, directing programs and camps, participating on judging teams and coaching them, and in promotional programs. Of all the honors I've received, the National 4-H Alumni Award makes me proudest.

A proud Orville displays his many 4-H Club ribbons.

☞ 9 ☜
Old Maids, Shy Fellows, and Popping Corn

I've been around popping corn all my life. Back when I was just knee-high to the nearest stalk, I learned that those kernels which just wouldn't pop no matter what, whether it was due to sheer orneriness or bad timing, were called Old Maids. It wasn't just our farm term; it was the industry term. Maybe it's not as fancy as some of the computer language they're developing out in Silicon Valley, but that's what it was.

Well, some seventy years later, I found myself on television talking about my Gourmet® Popping Corn and I used the words "Old Maids" to describe those unfulfilled kernels. Talk about bad timing. I got letters from a lot of angry ladies, who took offense at the term (Nina never much liked it either). I bow to their wishes. I now refer to those unpopped kernels as Shy Fellows, and the industry can proceed at its own risk!

Actually, I've done a lot of work to see that there are virtually no unpopped kernels in a batch of my Gourmet® Popping Corn, and if you and I have both done our jobs right, there shouldn't be any. But sometimes, just sometimes, a kernel or two does get pushed away from the heat it needs to pop. If that happens, put it back in the popper for the next batch.

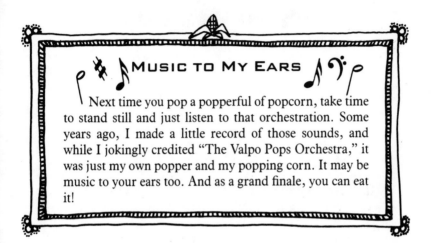

MUSIC TO MY EARS

Next time you pop a popperful of popcorn, take time to stand still and just listen to that orchestration. Some years ago, I made a little record of those sounds, and while I jokingly credited "The Valpo Pops Orchestra," it was just my own popper and my popping corn. It may be music to your ears too. And as a grand finale, you can eat it!

☛ 10 ☚
Popcorn and the New Wave

You can't get much more New Wave than the microwave oven. It's changing the way America cooks—though not what we eat.

There are specially designed microwave poppers on the market now and some specially designed popcorns for microwave ovens too. I like microwave convenience myself, but I noticed that sometimes microwave ovens don't have even heat distribution, and that means uneven results. Well, you're not going to tuck your microwave oven under your arm and take it back to the store for a different one because of that, and I wouldn't even suggest it, but the inconsistent quality and quantity of popcorn did bother me. I was dissatisfied, and you all know by now what happens when I get dissatisfied: I pop into action.

This time, I popped up with Orville Redenbacher's® Gourmet® Microwave Popping Corn in both Natural Flavor and Butter Flavor. I worked at it over a period of years before I was happy with it and sure that you would be too. It's made from the same premium hybrid as my Gourmet® Popping Corn.

You'll find my Gourmet® Microwave Popping Corn on your supermarket or grocer's shelves, right in the popcorn section where it belongs. What you get are prepackaged, specially designed bags that contain popping corn, oil, and salt. Not only is that convenient, but the bag has been expressly designed to hold in the heat and allow more even distribution than the oven might. You just tuck the bag in your microwave at the proper setting, sit back for 3 to 3½ minutes depending on the wattage of your microwave unit, and watch that bag expand as the popcorn pops. When it has finished with its popping, it's ready to eat, right out of the bag if you like. No muss, no fuss, no clean up.

My Gourmet® Microwave Popping Corn has the high-pop volume for which my brand is famous and the same good taste. I think the packaging is more convenient because it's shelf stable and features an easy eat-out-of-the-bag design. The bag is self-venting to allow the steam to escape so the popcorn won't get soggy. I wouldn't have it any other way.

One more advantage, as I said, is that you can just grab the bag out of the microwave, plop down with a good book or in front of the TV, and munch to your heart's content, right from the bag.

I'm sure you'll agree that there's nothing old-fashioned about the results of my Gourmet® Microwave Popping Corn—except for the great taste you've become accustomed to.

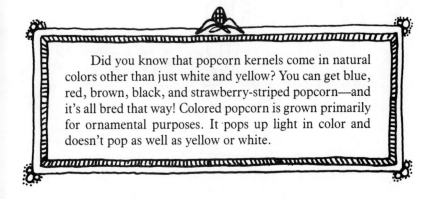

Did you know that popcorn kernels come in natural colors other than just white and yellow? You can get blue, red, brown, black, and strawberry-striped popcorn—and it's all bred that way! Colored popcorn is grown primarily for ornamental purposes. It pops up light in color and doesn't pop as well as yellow or white.

If you have a microwave, but have stocked up on my regular Gourmet® Popping Corn, don't worry! Here's a fun recipe that won't let your microwave go to waste.

Popcorn Haystacks

---

   1 qt. popped Orville Redenbacher's® Gourmet®
       Popping Corn
   1 cup peanuts
   1 (3-oz.) pkg. chow mein noodles
   1 (12-oz.) pkg. chocolate chips

Toss popped corn, peanuts, and chow mein noodles together in a large bowl. Set aside. Place chocolate chips in a glass bowl. Microwave on *medium high* for 3 minutes. Pour melted chips over popcorn mixture. Toss until well mixed. Place spoonfuls of the tossed mixture on waxed paper. Cool until firm. Store in a tightly covered container. Makes 24 haystacks.

☞ 11 ☜
Popcorn
Preservation

I've always believed that perfection should be preserved. In the case of my Gourmet® Popping Corn that's easy because it's packaged in resealable jars to keep the moisture content intact and the corn at its most poppable. All you have to do is keep the lid screwed on tight and put the jar on a cupboard shelf, but away from the stove. That's all. You don't have to store it in the refrigerator or in the freezer or in the coolest, darkest part of the cellar. In fact, doing those things isn't even good for the popcorn. (On the other hand, you don't want to get careless and leave the jar on the stove or on top of a radiator, either.) Just keep your unpopped popcorn in the jar, with the lid screwed on, and stowed away in a kitchen cupboard.

Now, with popped popcorn, you can get a bit more involved. If you're making a recipe for a party, say, probably the best way to serve it fresh and good-tasting is to pop it fresh. Actually, popping popcorn can be the highlight of a party— the guests can get involved in preparations and have fun too. No need to store the popcorn here!

If you're shipping the popcorn recipe off as a gift, you'll want a wrapping that's elegant and will also keep the popcorn fresh—a gift tin is perfect. In that case, Nina recommends lining your container with attractive cloth napkins or a nice bit of fabric before sealing it shut.

35

"Corn-crafts," such as popcorn balls and other types of preshaped clusters, also ship very well.

Some popcorn recipes ship better than others. Nina and I have put hours into developing recipes that withstand the rigors of the postal system. That's all part of being Popcorn King.

Sweet 'n' Crunchy Cereal Snack

    1 qt. popped Orville Redenbacher's® Gourmet®
        Popping Corn
 1/2 cup wheat germ
 1/2 cup sliced almonds, toasted
 1/4 cup shredded coconut, toasted
 1/4 cup butter
 1/2 cup sugar
    3 tbs. each: honey and water
 1/4 tsp. salt
 1/2 cup raisins

Mix popcorn, wheat germ, almonds, and coconut in a 9 × 13-inch buttered baking dish. Keep warm. In a large saucepan, melt butter; stir in sugar, honey, water, and salt. Cook over medium heat, stirring constantly, until mixture reaches 250° F on candy thermometer. Remove popcorn mixture from oven; stir in raisins. Pour syrup mixture over all; stir to coat. Bake at 250° F for 40–45 minutes, stirring occasionally. Spread on greased waxed paper to cool. Keep fresh in a tighly covered container. Makes approximately 6 cups of a tasty and healthy trail mix or TV snack.

Julia and William Redenbacher with their children—Mabel, Karl, Elsie, and Orville.

The American Mother deserves credit for helping spread popcorn overseas. She'd make cakes and cookies for sons and daughters in the Armed Forces, you see, and pack them in popped popcorn as protection. The sons and daughters, being no dummies, ate the packaging as well as the baked goods.

Orville's Poppin' Cake

   1 (16-oz.) pkg. miniature marshmallows
  1/4 cup butter
  1/2 tsp. vanilla
   5 qts. popped Orville Redenbacher's® Gourmet®
       Popping Corn
  1/2 cup jumbo cocktail peanuts

In double boiler, melt together marshmallows and butter; stir in vanilla. Pour over popcorn and peanuts. Mix well. Press into a well-greased spring bottom cake pan or Bundt cake pan. Turn out onto plate. Makes 1 cake.

Popcorn Party Mix

Popcorn Party Mix

¼ cup butter or margarine
½ tsp. garlic salt
½ tsp. onion salt
¼ tsp. celery salt
1½ tbs.Worcestershire
⅛ tsp. Tabasco
2 qts. popped Orville Redenbacher's® Gourmet®
    Popping Corn
1 cup pretzel sticks
1½ cups salted mixed nuts

Melt butter or margarine in a small saucepan. Add seasonings; mix thoroughly. Spread popcorn, pretzel sticks, and nuts in a large shallow baking pan. Pour seasoned butter over all; toss to mix. Bake at 275° F for 1 hour. Stir 4 or 5 times. Store in tightly covered container. Makes 2 quarts.

12

Campus Corn

It has, admittedly, been quite some years since I was a student at Purdue. But while my grandkids didn't tell me everything about their college careers, I do know a lot about what goes on in dormitories these days. And I can tell you that popping popcorn will always be a big part of campus life—social and otherwise.

With that in mind, Nina and I ensured the pop-ularity of our sixteen grandchildren when they were in college by providing them with popcorn, poppers, salt, oil, and toppings. Well, not only did they make friends more easily, but they reported that the popcorn got them through many a term paper and final exam. I'm not surprised. Some food experts may recommend fish or eggs or spinach as brain food, but I've always known that popcorn contains more than a few kernels of wisdom.

Popcorn is high in protein, low in calories. The sound of popcorn popping can wake you up energized, even at 3 A.M. And chewing on it exercises the jaw, which, for some reason, seems to exercise the brain, keeping the mind more alert.

I'm including several college-tested recipes here that can be made right in a dorm room without any special equipment other than a popper.

Pizza Popcorn

1/4 cup margarine
2 tsp. garlic salt
1/2 tsp. salt
1/2 tsp. oregano
2 qts. popped Orville Redenbacher's® Gourmet®
    Popping Corn
1/2 cup grated Parmesan cheese

Combine margarine, garlic salt, salt, and oregano in popper. Stir over low heat until blended (just pull the plug and let the heat die down a bit). Pour over popcorn while tossing gently. Sprinkle Parmesan cheese over and serve warm.

College Corn Bowl

---

1 tsp. chicken-flavored broth mix
1 tsp. water
1/2 tsp. poultry seasoning
1/2 tsp. celery seed
1/3 cup butter or margarine
4 qts. popped Orville Redenbacher's® Gourmet®
    Popping Corn

In a small saucepan, blend chicken broth mix, water, poultry seasoning, and celery seed until broth mix is dissolved. Add butter or margarine; melt over low heat. Keep mixture warm while preparing popcorn. Pour popped corn into a large serving bowl. Stir seasoned butter mixture; pour over popcorn and toss lightly but thoroughly. Serve at once. Makes 4-quarts.

Popcorn Rush

3 tbs. Wesson® Oil
½ cup Orville Redenbacher's® Gourmet® Popping Corn
½ cup powdered sugar
½ cup butter
2 tsp. cinnamon
1 tsp. salt
½ tsp. nutmeg
½ tsp. ground cloves

Heat oil in a 2-qt. popper; add popcorn. When corn is popped, empty into large bowl and sprinkle with powdered sugar. Melt butter in popper; add premeasured spices and stir to mix well. Pour over popcorn; toss until each kernel is coated. Serve immediately.*

---

*Wipe popper out with paper towels and repeat above procedure as many times as necessary.

☞ 13 ☜
I'm Game, Whatever the Name

Some people have trouble with my name, and I don't understand why. But they continually confuse me with Orville Wright, the man who flew the first airplane, and with Eddie Rickenbacker, the flying ace who served so well in World Wars I and II. I'm not either of those two fellows.

I do have some experience with flying, having visited some ninety-six countries in my lifetime (some of them weren't even countries when I began my lifetime!). The flying I've enjoyed best, though, has been in The Flying Kernel, my seven-story-high hot air balloon shaped like a piece of popped popcorn. The world's largest piece of popping corn, The Flying Kernel came about because I always said that the sky was the limit for my popping corn's potential and some folks countered by saying that I was full of hot air. I wasn't deflated by this, but back in 1977, when sales of Orville Redenbacher's® Gourmet® Popping Corn were soaring to number one, we launched the balloon to celebrate while still allowing those who scoffed to say, "See, I told you he was full of hot air!"

The Flying Kernel was the first hot air balloon to depart from traditional design and structure. It measures 70 feet high and 70 feet in diameter and contains about 85,000 cubic feet of air. Tom Oerman, who became our private pilot, always says,

The popcorn-shaped Orville Redenbacher® Gourmet® Popping Corn balloon, popularly known as the Flying Kernel.

"This baby's as light and fluffy as a cumulus cloud." That's what I always say about my popcorn, so we've got a good match.

Oerman also told me why balloonists invariably carry a couple bottles of champagne as ballast on their trips. It's not in case they get dry; it's a gift to appease those landlords on whose property they may unwittingly land in emergencies. Oerman now stocks my gourmet popping corn instead and he reports that it works just as well.

We took The Flying Kernel to the Kentucky Derby one year to compete in some balloon races. Nina, Tom, and I got inspired and popped up some special batches of popcorn for the occasion.

"Aunty Bellum" Flying Popcorn Balls

3 qts. popped Orville Redenbacher's® Gourmet® Popping Corn, unsalted
1 cup salted Spanish peanuts
1 (6-oz.) pkg. semi-sweet chocolate pieces
1 (1-lb.) pkg. marshmallows
1/4 cup butter or margarine

Combine popcorn, peanuts, and chocolate pieces in a large bowl or turkey roaster. In a large saucepan, cook marshmallows and butter or margarine over *low* heat until melted and smooth. Pour over popcorn mixture, tossing gently to mix well. Cool 5 minutes. Butter hands lightly. Form into 2½-inch balls. Makes about 15 balls.

Kentucky Praline Popcorn

4 qts. popped Orville Redenbacher's® Gourmet®
  Popping Corn, lightly salted
2 cups coarsely chopped pecans
3/4 cup butter or margarine
3/4 cup brown sugar, packed

In a large bowl or turkey roaster, mix popcorn and pecans. Combine butter or margarine and brown sugar in a small saucepan. Heat, stirring popcorn mixture. Mix well to coat popcorn evenly. Makes about 4 quarts.

Pegasus Popcorn

3 qts. popped Orville Redenbacher's® Gourmet®
  Popping Corn, lightly salted
1 cup chopped dried peaches
1 cup chopped dried apples
1 cup coarsely chopped walnuts
1/4 cup butter or margarine
3 tbs. sugar
1 tsp. cinnamon
1/2 tsp. nutmeg

In a large bowl or turkey roaster mix popcorn, fruits, and nuts. Combine butter or margarine, sugar, and spices in a small saucepan. Heat, stirring often, until butter is melted and sugar is dissolved. Pour over popcorn mixture. Toss gently to mix well. Makes about 3½ quarts.

☞ 14 ☜
Popcorn as Peacemaker

Popcorn has a peaceful effect on me. But I'm not the only one. There's even a historic precedent for it, going way back to the first Thanksgiving.

In gratitude for all the help they had received from the local Indians, the colonists invited them to join in that first Thanksgiving. It was a nice gesture, but there really wasn't that much food, so the Indians left for a bit and returned with a deer and fruit and nuts and things to stretch the meal for three full days. Quadequina, the chief's brother, brought a deerskin bag of popcorn as his goodwill offering and it was so well received that popcorn became a token of friendship at peace powwows too. Much healthier than those old pipes!

While a bowl of freshly popped popping corn usually does the trick for Nina and me, some folks and some situations need special treatment. The following recipes are almost guaranteed to placate and conciliate, no matter what the problem.

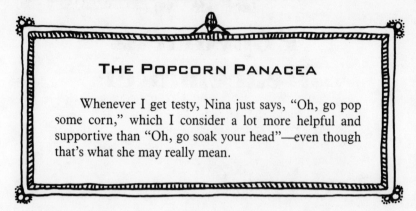

THE POPCORN PANACEA

Whenever I get testy, Nina just says, "Oh, go pop some corn," which I consider a lot more helpful and supportive than "Oh, go soak your head"—even though that's what she may really mean.

Peacemaker's Mousse

3 cups popped Orville Redenbacher's® Gourmet® Popping Corn
½ cup chopped pecans
¼ lb. vanilla caramels (about 14)
1 tbs. water
3 cups whipping cream
¼ cup sugar
¼ cup peach-flavored brandy or Cointreau
1 cup chopped canned peaches

Keep popcorn and pecans hot in 300°F oven. Combine caramels and water in a heavy saucepan; melt slowly, stirring frequently. In a bowl, toss melted caramel with popcorn and nuts. Cool; coarsely chop. Whip cream until stiff; blend in sugar and brandy. Fold in peaches and ⅔ of popcorn mixture; pour into 2-qt. mold. Freeze until firm. Unmold and garnish top with remaining popcorn mixture.

Honey Buns

8 tsp. honey
1 cup finely ground popped Orville Redenbacher's®
   Gourmet® Popping Corn
1 (12-oz) pkg. refrigerated dinner rolls
1 tsp. cinnamon
¼ cup halved maraschino cherries

Preheat oven to 350°F. Butter an 8-cup muffin tin. Mix honey and ground popcorn. Divide mixture evenly in muffin cups. Unwrap dinner roll dough and sprinkle with cinnamon. Fold edges of each roll over cinnamon, forming bun shapes. Place seam sides down over popcorn and honey in muffin cups. Bake for 20 minutes or until tops are brown. Place buns upside down on serving dish. Garnish with cherry halves. Serve hot. Makes 8 muffins.

The Elegance and Etiquette of Popcorn

The Victorians were crazy about popping corn, and they went so far as to create rituals around it, singing little ditties and putting their recipes in verse form and so on.

Back in the Victorian era, popcorn was trickier to eat than it is today. One encountered more "shy fellows" and bits of husk, hull, and cob—this was long before my Gourmet® Popping Corn, remember! And as you can well imagine, toothpicks were pretty much essential. In those days, etiquette books were filled with advice on how to wield them discreetly.

Eating popcorn may have been a nuisance back then, but even the comparatively bad popcorn available was better than no popcorn at all. Nowadays, with popcorn much improved and my Gourmet® Popping Corn as close to perfect as possible, the only rules of etiquette to follow are few and simple:

1. Leave some for the next guy; it's easy to make more.
2. Keep your elbows to yourself.
3. If you are host or hostess at a party where popcorn is served, never pass the bowl without the comforting assurance that "there's more where this came from!"

So much for etiquette.

50

Sister Mabel's Caramel Corn (see recipe, page 27)

As for elegance, it didn't die with the Victorian era, no matter what some people say. There are plenty of elegant things to do with popcorn even today.

For instance, you can use popcorn in place of croutons in green salads, which looks quite nice and makes a conversation starter as well. The same holds true for floating popcorn in soups. (I find it especially good in cheddar cheese soup and cream of tomato. Chili too.)

Nina often just provides guests with individual trays holding a popcorn bowl, salt or other seasoning, and a pretty washcloth, slightly dampened for cleaning up. That's a tasteful touch, and it seems to be much appreciated.

And if that's not enough, here are some especially elegant recipes to dazzle and delight guests of any age, Victorian or otherwise.

Popcorn Stuffing Balls

¼ cup butter
¼ cup chopped onion
¼ cup chopped celery
1 beef bouillon cube
1 cup boiling water
5 cups popped Orville Redenbacher's® Gourmet® Popping Corn
1 cup seasoned stuffing crumbs
1 cup diced apples, peeled
¼ cup dark raisins

Melt butter in skillet; add onion and celery, and cook until tender. Dissolve bouillon cube in boiling water; stir in with onion and celery mixture. Add popcorn, stuffing crumbs, apples, and raisins; toss well. Form mixture into 2½-inch balls and place on buttered baking sheet. Place in oven with pork roast or chops during last half hour of baking time. When serving, arrange popcorn balls around meat on platter. Makes 10 balls.

Seasoned Fish Fillets

1 lb. white fish fillets
2 tbs. butter, melted
1/2 cup finely ground popped Orville Redenbacher's®
     Gourmet® Popping Corn
1 tsp. seasoned salt
1/2 tsp. dill weed
1/4 tsp. pepper

Brush both sides of fish fillets with butter and arrange on broiler pan. In a small bowl combine remaining ingredients. Sprinkle half of the popcorn mixture evenly over fish. Broil 6 inches from heat for 5–10 minutes. Remove fish from oven. Turn, sprinkle with remaining popcorn mixture, and broil for 5–10 minutes longer. Makes 4 servings.

Smoky Parmesan Toss

1/2 cup butter or margarine, melted
1/2 tsp. onion salt
1/2 tsp. hickory-smoked salt
1/4 cup bacon bits
4 qts. popped Orville Redenbacher's® Gourmet®
     Popping Corn
1/2 cup grated Parmesan cheese

Add onion salt, hickory-smoked salt, and bacon bits to butter; mix well. Toss lightly but thoroughly with freshly popped Orville Redenbacher's® Gourmet® Popping Corn. Sprinkle with Parmesan cheese; toss again. Makes 4 quarts of popcorn.

☞ 16 ☜
Healthy Snacking

I like the way historians put names to decades, don't you? I don't always remember the era as being that way, but the titles are tidy. The 1920s were Roaring, and the thirties were Depressed. In the sixties we Flowered, and in the seventies we got Fit. Or fit to be tied with trying to.

Seems like everyone was making a cult of Health Consciousness in the 1970s. Now, I enjoy good health and hope to keep on enjoying it for another decade or two, but I think things got carried away. It's been organic-this and organic-that everywhere, and it all costs a lot too. A lot of folks spent their money and some even ate the stuff that was labeled as good for them no matter how bad it tasted—or they felt guilty if they didn't. Which was just as bad.

Snack foods, or fun foods, were especially under suspicion. I guess it goes back to the old theory that medicine has to taste bad to be good for you.

In the case of popcorn, you'll be glad to know, you don't need to sneak to snack. Popcorn is a whole grain, it's excellent roughage without roughing it, and it aids digestion. And one cup of unbuttered popcorn has fewer calories than half a medium grapefruit or a portion of cottage cheese.

Popcorn is good for you. There's just nothing bad about it. And it's inexpensive, too, at pennies per serving. Maybe it will help the eighties to become known as The Age of Enlightened Eating.

Nature's Own Puffed Breakfast Cereal

¼ cup light brown sugar
1 tbs. Orville Redenbacher's® Gourmet® Buttery
Flavor® Popping Oil
1 tbs. water
½ tsp. vanilla
⅛ tsp. cinnamon
4 qts. popped Orville Redenbacher's® Gourmet®
Popping Corn

Combine sugar, oil, water, vanilla, and cinnamon in a small bowl. Place popped corn in a large bowl. Drizzle sugar mixture over popped corn; toss until all is coated. Spread coated popped corn on a large shallow baking sheet. Bake at 300°F for 15 minutes, or until desired crispness. Store in a tightly covered container or sealed plastic bag. Makes approximately 4 quarts.

This popcorn cereal has fewer calories per serving than other presweetened cereals and is also low in sodium.

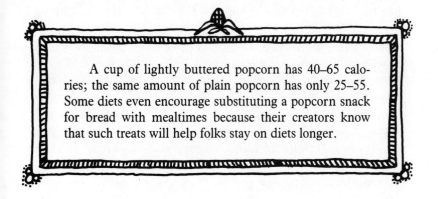

A cup of lightly buttered popcorn has 40–65 calories; the same amount of plain popcorn has only 25–55. Some diets even encourage substituting a popcorn snack for bread with mealtimes because their creators know that such treats will help folks stay on diets longer.

☞ 17 ☜
The Butter Battle

Okay, okay. I know some of you are firmly entrenched in the trends of the times and you're sneering, "Sure, popcorn is good for you, but what about all the butter people pour on?"

Well, you're right. Butter means many extra calories, plus cholesterol, and expense, and probably a lot of other stuff that folks just don't need. But then, good popcorn doesn't need butter.

I happen to be a popcorn purist, and I most often eat mine with just a bit of popcorn salt to bring out the flavor. There are recipes in this book that don't use butter either.

I realize, though, that for some folks popcorn without butter is just not worth its salt. That's why I've come out with Orville Redenbacher's® Gourmet® Buttery Flavor® Popping Oil. It gives popped corn the taste, aroma, and color of butter, but without the mess, cholesterol, and calories that butter brings to any dish. (It also makes hand-holding easier to get a grip on. Maybe the 1980s could herald the Return of Romance?)

Anyway, it's a "butter" way to pop, butterlessly, and Nina, my health conscience, also uses it for sautéing, pan frying, stir frying, griddle cooking, and anywhere else we might ordinarily use other cooking oils. Calorically speaking, you might say it's a case of "Waist not, want not."

All weights = 100 grams (3½ oz.)

	Calories	Protein grams	Carbohydrate grams	Fiber grams	Fat grams	Calcium milligrams	Phosphorus milligrams	Iron milligrams	Thiamine milligrams	Riboflavin milligrams	Niacin milligrams	Ascorbic Acid milligrams	Vitamin A International Units
Plain popcorn, popped	386	12.7	76.7	2.2	5.0	11*	281*	2.7*	—	.12	2.2	0*	—
Popcorn, popped with salt and oil	456	9.8	59.1	1.7	21.8	8	216	2.1	—	.09	1.7	0	—
Potato chips, plain	568	5.3	50.0	1.6*	39.8	40	139	1.8	.21	.07	4.8	16	TR
Ice cream cones	377	10.0	77.9	.2	2.4	156	198	.4	.05	.21	.5	TR	TR
Pretzels	390	9.8	75.9	.3	4.5	22	131	1.5	.02	.03	.7	0*	0*
Saltines	433	9.0	71.5	.4	12.0	21	90	1.2	.01	.04	1.0	0*	0*

*Values imputed from another form of the food or from a similar food; zero indicates that the amount of the constituent is probably none or is too small to measure.

Source: *Composition of Foods—Raw, Processed, Prepared,* Agriculture Handbook No. 8, United States Department of Agriculture.

How to Make
Popcorn Blush, and
Other Party Tricks

There's something about popcorn—the sound of it and the smell of it and the anticipated taste of it—that just makes people more convivial. They relax, they let go of their tensions, they get in a party mood. I think popcorn works better than martinis for making folks friendly. It's like a little bit of magic.

You can conjure up some pretty impressive party dishes with it too. For instance, when my granddaughter Pam was just a tyke, and not yet the beautiful young woman she's become, she demanded pink popcorn for a birthday celebration. (It was challenges like that one that turned my hair silver.) I thought her faith in me was touching, and I didn't want to let her down—and my honor was at stake—so I went

Pink Birthday Party Pie

58

to a friend and explained the problem. That great lady came up with a recipe that we've used now for years and even made into a crust for Pam's birthday pie.

Pink Birthday Party Pie

---

    ³/₄ cup granulated sugar
    ¹/₄ cup light corn syrup
    1 tbs. butter
    ¹/₄ tsp. salt
    ¹/₈ tsp. cream of tartar
    1–2 tbs. strawberry-flavored gelatin
    ¹/₂ tsp. baking soda
    1 qt. popped Orville Redenbacher's® Gourmet®
        Popping Corn
    1 qt. French vanilla ice cream, slightly softened
        fresh strawberries, halved, for garnish

Combine sugar, corn syrup, butter, salt, and cream of tartar in a 1-qt. saucepan. Bring to boil, stirring constantly. Cook without stirring, to 250° F on candy thermometer (hard ball stage).* Stir in strawberry-flavored gelatin; continue cooking about 1 minute to 260° F. Remove from heat. Add baking soda and stir quickly but thoroughly. Pour at once while foamy over popped corn in a bowl; mix gently to coat thoroughly. Press, with lightly buttered fingers, onto bottom and sides of a buttered 9–10-inch pie pan. Bake at 200° F for 45 minutes. Cool. Fill with ice cream, spreading smooth with back of spoon. Arrange strawberry halves cut side down in pattern over top. Serve at once or freeze until ready to serve.† Makes 6 servings.

---

*Hard ball stage—when boiling syrup dropped into very cold water forms a hard ball.

†When freezing pie, do not add strawberries until just before serving.

☞ NINA'S HINTS FOR OTHER SPECIAL OCCASIONS

Use the same recipe as above, with these variations depending on the occasion!

Valentine's Day Party. Use raspberry-flavored gelatin; press onto bottom and sides of buttered heart-shaped mold before baking. Cool and fill with raspberry sherbet. Decorate with poufs of whipped cream.

Halloween Party. Use orange-flavored gelatin; fill baked and cooled pie shell with chocolate ice cream. Garnish with whipped cream and sprinkle with confetti cake decorations.

Christmas Party. Use cherry-flavored gelatin; prepare popcorn crust in Christmas mold if desired. Cool and fill with pistachio ice cream. Garnish with whipped cream and a sprinkle of red or green fine cake decorating candy crystals.

Popcorn Pastels

You might want to try simply popping up a batch of Popcorn Pastels—they add a festive touch to a holiday gathering of any season.

Popcorn Pastels

4 qts. popped Orville Redenbacher's® Gourmet® Popping Corn
1½ cups granulated sugar
½ cup light corn syrup
2 tbs. butter
½ tsp. salt
¼ tsp. cream of tartar
3–4 tbs. any flavor gelatin dessert
1 tsp. baking soda

Keep freshly popped corn warm in a large baking pan in oven at 200°F. In medium saucepan, combine sugar, corn syrup, butter, salt, and cream of tartar. Bring to boil, stirring constantly. Cook to 250°F on candy thermometer (hard ball stage)* without stirring. Stir in flavored gelatin; continue cooking about 1 minute to 260°F. Remove from heat. Add baking soda and stir in quickly but thoroughly. Pour at once while foamy over warm popcorn; mix gently to coat corn. Return to oven; bake at 200°F for 1 hour. Stir two or three times. Cool completely. Separate into small pieces. Store in tightly covered containers. Makes 4 quarts.

---

*Hard ball stage—when boiling syrup dropped into very cold water forms a hard ball.

The Harvest Pumpkin Ball is my personal favorite popcorn party decoration because it's so handsome—and so edible! We usually have one out at Halloween for guests.

Harvest Pumpkin Ball

1/4 cup water
1 tsp. pumpkin pie spice
1/4 tsp. salt
1 lb. vanilla caramels (about 64)
4 qts. popped Orville Redenbacher's® Gourmet® Popping Corn
    shoestring licorice
    green gumdrops

Combine water, pumpkin pie spice, and salt in top of double boiler; mix well. Add caramels; melt over hot water, stirring often, until smooth. Pour mixture over popped corn in a large bowl; toss until kernels are well coated. With lightly buttered hands, form into pumpkin shape measuring about 8 inches in diameter at the bottom and about 4½ inches high at the center. Make 7 or 8 slight indentations from center to bottom to form pumpkin "sections." Cut strips of shoestring licorice and press down center of each indentation. Use green gumdrops to make pumpkin "stem." Arrange with cornucopia of fresh red and green apples, grapes, and nuts and use as the centerpiece for your table.

Among the traditional treats of Halloween are big crunchy Popcorn Balls wrapped in bright orange and black cellophane. These are an easy-to-prepare variation of Sister Mabel's Caramel Corn (see page 27). We give them to trick-or-treaters; they're real spirit raisers!

Orville and friend prepare for Halloween with Spirit-raising Popcorn Balls and Harvest Pumpkin Ball.

Spirit-raising Popcorn Balls

Prepare Caramel Corn recipe. Butter hands; shape mixture into 3-inch balls and place on waxed paper. Store in tightly covered containers. Makes approximately 1 dozen.

A lot of the recipes in this book have that special effect on folks, but just-plain-popcorn can also do the trick. Let 'em measure and pour, and pass the napkins and bowls—and you'll see.

☞ 19 ☜
Pajama Popcorn

When my daughters were growing up, they used to hold a lot of Slumber Parties. I never understood why they were called that because no one ever got any sleep (including me! How could anyone sleep with all that giggling going on?). Anyway, they liked the parties and now their kids do, too, although I believe the more popular term now is Pajama Parties, which makes a whole lot more sense to me as names go.

Popcorn is especially appropriate at Pajama Parties: it is fun and it is festive—and it's hard to giggle while you're eating it. You might want to make up large batches of the following recipes; they'll help bring the noise level down to a pleasant "Mmmmmmmmmm."

Chocolate Chew-Chews

    2 tbs. milk
    1 tbs. butter
   24 chocolate caramels
    8 vanilla caramels
   1/4 tsp. salt
    1 qt. popped Orville Redenbacher's® Gourmet®
          Popping Corn
    1 cup granola
   1/2 cup golden raisins
   1/2 cup dry roasted cashew nuts, chopped coarsely

Combine milk, butter, chocolate and vanilla caramels, and salt in top part of a double boiler. Melt over hot water, stirring until smooth and creamy. In a large bowl, combine popped corn, granola, raisins, and nuts. Add melted chocolate mixture: stir to mix thoroughly. Drop by teaspoonfuls on ungreased cookie sheet. Bake at 200°F for 15 minutes. Allow to cool completely before removing from pan. Makes approximately 54 clusters.

Winter Warmer

Seasoned and spiced popcorn can warm up any night. Prepare the spice "pop-pourri" by combining 6 tablespoons salt, 2 teaspoons paprika, 1 teaspoon dry mustard, and 1/2 teaspoon each of garlic salt, celery salt, thyme, marjoram, curry powder, and dill weed. Mix well or blend in an electric blender. This makes 1/2 cup. Use 3 tablespoons Winter Warmer to season 3 quarts unsalted popped Orville Redenbacher's® Gourmet® Popping Corn. Store the remainder in a covered jar.

Bedtime Brittle

Bedtime Brittle

2 qts. popped Orville Redenbacher's® Gourmet®
   Popping Corn
$1/2$ cup dry roasted peanuts
1 cup sugar
$1/2$ cup corn syrup
$1/2$ cup water
2 tbs. molasses
2 tbs. butter or margarine
1 tsp. vinegar
1 tsp. baking soda

Combine popcorn and nuts and place in a buttered
9 × 13 × 2-inch pan. In a separate heavy saucepan, combine
sugar, corn syrup, water, molasses, butter or margarine, and
vinegar. Stir mixture while heating until sugar is dissolved.
Then cook over medium heat, without stirring, until mixture
reaches 300°F on candy thermometer (hard crack stage).*
Remove from heat. Add baking soda, stirring in quickly only
enough to mix. Pour immediately over popcorn and nuts and
toss to coat.

Turn mixture out onto a large buttered surface. With two
forks, pull apart into pieces as thin as possible. Let cool, then
break into smaller pieces. Makes approximately 2 quarts.

---

*Hard crack stage—when boiling syrup dropped into very cold water
forms hard threads that, upon removal from the water, are brittle.

☞ 20 ☜

Popcorn and the Picture Show

Popcorn and movies go together like hands clasping during romantic scenes.

This famous twosome first got together—or at least pretty close—in Chicago at the 1893 Columbian Exposition. Thomas Alva Edison was in one of the exhibition buildings showing off his new movie projector, and Charles Cretors was somewhere outside, showing off his popcorn popping machine and feeding the crowds.

Before long, both were established—there were movie theaters everywhere (called Nickelodeons because that's what they cost and that shows you how long ago we're talking about!) and there were popcorn concessions too. The popcorn concessions were manned from popcorn wagons, however, parked way down the street from the theaters. The theater owners wanted no part of the noisypopping snack.

As Nickelodeons turned into Moving Picture Palaces and got more and more elaborate in decor, they shunned popcorn even more. Going to the movies was meant to be an elegant experience, and popcorn was still noisy and messy for theater owners to clean up. They just didn't want it at all.

Moviegoers didn't agree. They continued to buy their popcorn down the block and sneak it into the theater with them. The owners could see that the popcorn vendors were

67

making piles of money, but they stood fast in their ban . . . until the Great Depression of the 1930s. Those were hard times and some people stopped going to the movies, but they still patronized the popcorn vendors and sometimes made popcorn their main meal of the day.

Smart operators bought poppers and moved them right into the lobbies of the theaters, where they are positioned today. It was the extra plus of popcorn that kept a good many movie houses in business during those hard times and a good many moving picture companies likewise.

According to statistics, movie house popcorn sales are best when comedies are on the screen. Action movies are next; then dramas; and, lastly, romances.

An old-fashioned popcorn wagon

☛ 21 ☚
Tops for TV Too!

According to The Popcorn Institute (and no one knows better than they do!) some 30 percent of the popcorn sold today is eaten outside the home—in movie theaters, stadiums, schools, and the like. The remaining 70 percent is eaten in the home. And while they don't go on to say so, I'd bet that a lot of that 70 percent is eaten in front of the TV.

I myself enjoy TV most when I have a bowl of popcorn at hand and a kernel or two in mouth. I have noticed, however, that the type of show I've tuned in to seems to dictate the type of popcorn I want to dig into. Maybe it's the same with you.

Newscasts, it seems to me, require a sweet recipe to kind of balance the souring effect the news of the day can have. Talk shows, for which I have to admit a personal predilection, need a quiet-eating popcorn so I won't miss one kernel of wisdom that a guest may let drop. Variety shows call for a mixed dish, maybe something with some peanuts or pretzels in it; sportscasts cry for a macho recipe with a bit of bite to it; and situation comedies should be watched with my pure popcorn because it's hard to laugh with your mouth full and you want to be able to take just a kernel or two at a time. If you're addicted to the soap operas, you might do well with an onion-flavored recipe so you can blame the tears on that.

You'll find plenty of recipes in this book and I'm sure you'll pick some personal favorites for your favorite TV shows. Here are a few other Pop Tops to go on with in the meantime.

All My Popcorn—Soap Opera Snack

4 qts. popped Orville Redenbacher's® Gourmet® Popping Corn
1/3 cup butter or margarine, melted
1/2 tsp. each garlic and onion salt
2 cups shredded sharp Cheddar cheese

Empty popped corn into an ovenproof mixing bowl. Add margarine, salts, and cheese (a small amount at a time), and toss. Place in a 325°F oven for 5–10 minutes to melt cheese; stir gently once or twice. Makes 4 quarts.

Five o'Clock News Pop

1/4 cup powdered sugar
1/4 cup brown sugar, packed
1/2 tsp. imitation butter-flavored salt
1/2 tsp. nutmeg
1 tsp. dry orange peel bits
1/2 tsp. dry lemon peel bits

Sift powdered sugar, brown sugar, salt, and nutmeg together into a small bowl. Add orange and lemon peel bits; mix thoroughly. Store in a shaker with several large hole openings. Sprinkle, as desired, on freshly popped Orville Redenbacher's® Gourmet® Popping Corn.

Spice of Life Popcorn

---

¹/₃ cup grated Romano cheese
1 (about ¹/₂-oz.) pkg. garlic-flavored dip mix
2 tsp. paprika

Combine grated cheese, dip mix, and paprika in small bowl; mix thoroughly. Store in a shaker with several large hole openings. Sprinkle, as desired, on freshly popped Orville Redenbacher's® Gourmet® Popping Corn.

Spice of Life Popcorn

Popcorn of Champions

---

¹/₄ cup popcorn salt
2 tsp. chili powder
1 tsp. paprika
1 tsp. imitation butter-flavored salt
¹/₃ tsp. onion powder

Sift all ingredients together into a small bowl until well blended. Store in a shaker with several large hole openings. Sprinkle, as desired, on freshly popped Orville Redenbacher's® Gourmet® Popping Corn.

☞ 22 ☜
Popcorn and the Good Sport

I happen to enjoy sports, and of all sports I enjoy football most even though I earned my Purdue letterman's sweaters in Big 10 Competition in track and cross-country events. My favorite team is Purdue, my alma mater, and I'm glad to say that their games are most often well worth watching.

Part of the pleasure, for me at least, is sitting out in the stands, halfway to freezing sometimes, and cheering myself hoarse. When I can't get to the game, I join the huddle at the TV set, like everyone else.

Now you may not have noticed this, and possibly most people wouldn't, but there are a lot of similarities between the action at a football game (Bowl games and otherwise) and the action at a popcorn bowl. Maybe it's because they're both All-American. Be that as it may, here are some recipes that are bound to make a big score with popcorn fans.

Benchwarmer Bars

1 cup soft butter or margarine
1 (14-oz.) can sweetened condensed milk
1 tsp. vanilla
2 cups flaked coconut
½ cup finely ground walnuts
4 qts. popped Orville Redenbacher's® Gourmet®
    Popping Corn
1 (6-oz.) pkg. semi-sweet chocolate pieces

In a large mixing bowl, cream butter; beat in condensed milk and vanilla. Stir in coconut and walnuts. Pour mixture over popped corn in a large bowl or roasting pan; stir gently until all kernels are coated. Press firmly into 9 × 13 × 2-inch pan. Melt chocolate over very low heat; drizzle over popcorn mixture to form lacy pattern. Refrigerate until firm, about 4 hours. Cut into 1½ × 2-inch bars. Makes about 3 dozen.

Benchwarmer Bars

Sideliner's Snack

6 qts. popped Orville Redenbacher's® Gourmet®
　　Popping Corn
4 cups corn chips
2 cups stick pretzels
1 (4-oz.) can diced green chilis
½ cup butter or margarine, melted
1½ tsp. seasoned salt
2 cups shredded Cheddar cheese

In a large shallow baking pan, combine popped corn, corn chips, pretzels, chilis, butter, and salt; toss gently. Sprinkle with cheese; bake at 350°F for 10 minutes or until cheese melts. Makes about 7½ quarts.

Punt and Pass Popcorn

4 qts. popped Orville Redenbacher's® Gourmet®
　　Popping Corn
3 tbs. butter or margarine, melted
¼ cup grated Parmesan cheese
2 tbs. (about ½ pkg.) spaghetti sauce mix without
　　mushrooms
½ tsp. leaf oregano
2 ozs. thin pepperoni slices, halved
1 (4½-oz.) jar sliced mushrooms, well drained
1 (2-oz.) jar pimiento-stuffed green olives, sliced

Place popped corn in a 6-quart (or larger) bowl or roasting pan. Drizzle with melted butter. Sprinkle with cheese, spaghetti sauce mix, and oregano; toss gently. Add pepperoni, mushrooms, and olives; mix well. Makes about 4 quarts.

Sideliner's Snack

Quarterback Crunch

5 qts. popped Orville Redenbacher's® Gourmet®
     Popping Corn
2 cups miniature marshmallows
1 cup whole roasted almonds
2 cups light brown sugar firmly packed
¹/₂ cup light corn syrup
¹/₂ lb. butter or margarine
¹/₄ tsp. cream of tartar
1 tsp. salt
1 tsp. baking soda

In a large roasting or baking pan, combine popped corn, marshmallows, and almonds; set aside. In a 2¹/₂-quart saucepan, combine brown sugar, corn syrup, butter or margarine, cream of tartar, and salt. Bring to a boil, stirring over medium high heat. Stirring constantly, boil rapidly to hard ball stage,★ 260° F on candy thermometer (about 5 minutes). Remove from heat. Stir in baking soda quickly but thoroughly; pour immediately over popcorn mixture. Stir gently until well coated. Turn out at once on wax paper; spread apart and allow to cool completely. Break apart; store in airtight container. Makes about 6 quarts.

★Hard ball stage—when boiling syrup dropped into very cold water forms a hard ball.

☛ 23 ☜
On the Outs with Popcorn

I've always been an outdoorsy sort of man. I used to do a lot of camping—backpacking, getting out in the wilderness, or even out into the back forty when I couldn't get any farther. In any case, I know that careful planning is essential when preparing for a back-to-nature journey, whether by land or by sea, and popcorn has always been a part of my plans.

That's only natural. After all, popcorn is lightweight, compact, packable, portable, economical, and nutritious. And good! Because "good" has always been a priority with me, I worked out a couple of recipes that are easy to tame even in the wild.

The first recipe, Smoky Popcorn, is appealing for campers and backpackers who have to keep both their equipment and foodstuffs to the essential minimum. The breakfast bacon or sausage will provide enough drippings for you to pop the corn, and you can do it right in the same pan if you've got a good cover for it.

And the topping for Barbecued Popcorn can be made up before you leave home and just sprinkled over your popping corn once you hit the great out-of-doors. (Even if it's only next door.)

Smoky Popcorn

3–4 slices bacon*
½ cup Orville Redenbacher's® Gourmet® Popping
   Corn
Smoky flavored salt

Cube bacon and place in a heavy 12-inch skillet over medium high heat (or on a grill over campfire coals). Cook, stirring, until bacon fat cooks out enough to coat bottom of skillet. If necessary, pour off excess fat. Add popcorn; stir and mix well.

Cover skillet loosely (so that some steam can escape); shake skillet back and forth until corn starts popping. Continue to shake skillet until popping slows down, then remove from heat or to edge of grill until corn finishes popping. Season with smoky flavored salt to taste. Makes about 4 quarts popcorn.

NOTE: Do not attempt to duplicate this recipe in an electric popper.

---

*5 or 6 pork sausage links may be diced and used in place of bacon.

Smoky Popcorn

Barbecued Popcorn

2 tsp. dried parsley flakes
2 tsp. paprika
1/2 tsp. hickory smoked salt
1/2 tsp. onion powder
1/4 tsp. garlic powder
2 qts. popped Orville Redenbacher's® Gourmet®
    Popping Corn

Combine dried ingredients. Pour over freshly popped popcorn. Toss gently.

☞ 24 ☜
I Get a Little Corny at Christmas

Some people think there's something corny about the idea of an old-fashioned Christmas. My answer to that is a firm "Bah, humbug!"

Granted, family and friends are scattered all over the globe, but we make an effort to keep in touch and to get together whenever we can. Christmas is a time when we try even harder, and even when we can't be with the folks we care about we can share the holidays with them by mail. Nina has me beating a path to the post office with the Della Robbia Popcorn Bowl gift packages—they ship real well.

See page 86 for recipe for Christmas Snowman.

Della Robbia Popcorn Bowl

1 cup mixed dried fruit (apricots, prunes, peaches,
   and pears), cut in bite-size pieces
¼ cup golden seedless raisins
1 cup dry-roasted mixed nuts
3 qts. freshly popped Orville Redenbacher's®
   Gourmet® Popping Corn
popcorn salt (optional)

In a large bowl, toss dried fruit, raisins, and nuts with freshly popped corn. Sprinkle lightly with popcorn salt, if desired. Serve. Makes about 3½ quarts.

Anyway, I like Christmas and I like traditions. I also like creating new traditions. It's never too late. As you'll recall, the popcorn hybrid I use for my Gourmet® Popping Corn is the Snowflake variety, and that makes it real appropriate for incorporating into our festivities.

We always have our Christmas Snowman (though his hat is old-hat now and needs replacing) and our Popcorn Candle Holders. Nina makes a Della Robbia Wreath for the mantel as well as Della Robbia gift packs to send. We make popcorn balls and popcorn nosegays and popcorn garlands, and anything else we can think of. If that's corny, so be it.

Della Robbia Wreath

4 qts. Orville Redenbacher's® Gourmet® Popping
     Corn
2 cups granulated sugar
¹/₂ cup light corn syrup
¹/₄ cup water
2 tbs. butter
¹/₂ tsp. cream of tartar
¹/₂ tsp. salt
1 (3-oz.) pkg. lime-flavored gelatin
1 tsp. baking soda
     12″ or 14″ styrofoam ring
     fruit-shaped marzipan candies, candy leaves,
         berries, ribbon

Keep freshly popped corn warm in a large baking pan in oven at 200° F. In a medium saucepan, combine sugar, corn syrup, 2 tablespoons water, butter, cream of tartar, and salt. Bring to a boil, stirring constantly. Cook to 290° F on candy thermometer (hard crack stage)★ without stirring. Mix flavored gelatin with 2 tablespoons hot water. Stir into hot syrup; remove from heat. *Reserve about ¹/₄ cup syrup* to use in *attaching* decorations; keep warm over remaining hot water. Add baking soda to *remaining* syrup and stir in quickly but thoroughly. Pour at once while foamy over warm popcorn; mix gently to coat corn. Return to 200° F oven for 30 minutes; stir occasionally. While mixture is warm, shape onto styrofoam ring to form a wreath. Decorate as desired with candy, fruits, and leaves, using reserved syrup to hold decorations in place. Cool completely. Tie ribbon through wreath to hang. Makes 1 wreath.

★Hard crack stage—when boiling syrup dropped into very cold water forms hard threads that, upon removal from the water, are brittle.

Orville and his wife, Nina, celebrate the Christmas holidays with decorations using popping corn.

Popcorn Star and Garlands

---

4 qts. popped Orville Redenbacher's® Gourmet®
Popping Corn
2 cups sugar
1 cup corn syrup
½ cup water
½ cup salt
¼ tsp. peppermint extract

Keep freshly popped corn warm in a large baking pan in oven at 200°. In a heavy ½-qt. saucepan, combine sugar, corn syrup, water, and salt. Bring to a boil, stirring. Boil, without stirring, to 290°F on candy thermometer (hard crack stage).* Remove from heat; stir in peppermint extract. Pour over popped corn, stirring gently to coat kernels. Return to oven to keep mixture easy to handle.

STAR
Take out a portion of mixture and form into a flat star shape on a *foil-covered cardboard pattern* 6–8 inches in diameter. (Insert a 10–12-inch-long *wooden dowel* halfway up star pattern to use to secure star to top of tree.) Press gently to star shape; cool until firm.

GARLANDS
Take out additional popcorn mixture from oven, a small amount at a time, and separate into two or three kernel clusters on foil or waxed paper. Cool until firm. String on *coarse white thread,* or doubled waxed thread, using a *strong needle.*

---

*Hard crack stage—when boiling syrup dropped into very cold water forms hard threads that, upon removal from the water, are brittle.

Popcorn Ball Ornaments

BASIC MARSHMALLOW MIXTURE FOR 4 QUARTS POPPED CORN

½ cup butter or margarine
1 (10½-oz.) bag miniature marshmallows
1 tsp. vanilla, almond, or peppermint flavoring
¼ tsp. salt
    food coloring (optional)

BALL ORNAMENTS

Combine butter and marshmallows in a heavy saucepan. Melt together over low heat, stirring until mixture is smooth and well blended. Stir in flavoring, salt, and a few drops of food coloring, if desired. Pour over 4 quarts popped Orville Redenbacher's® Gourmet® Popping Corn in a large bowl; mix gently until kernels are well coated. With lightly buttered hands, form into balls of desired size. Insert hanger loops or small candy canes (peel wrappers back from ends of cane). Decorate as desired. Wrap cooled balls in squares of cellophane; fasten with a twister seal, and tie with a ribbon bow at top, just below hanger.

NOSEGAY ORNAMENTS

Prepare another basic marshmallow mixture as above; divide as desired and stir in several drops of food coloring to tint. Stir one color mixture over a portion of popped Orville Redenbacher's® Gourmet® Popping Corn; mix well. Repeat with other colors. Form into small five or six kernel clusters around pipe cleaners; place on waxed paper to dry. Gather into nosegays; push ends of pipe cleaners through center of 4-inch paper doilies; secure with wire or twister seal, looped for handling. Add bowed ribbon streamers. Makes approximately 16 ornaments.

DECORATIONS

Small candy canes, cord loops, wire twister seals, or pipe cleaners for hanging; cake decorations, colored sugar crystals, fruit-flavored gum drops; cellophane or clear wrap; ribbons, paper doilies

Basic Syrup Mixture for 4 Quarts Popped Corn

2 cups granulated sugar
1/2 cup light corn syrup
2 tbs. water
2 tbs. butter
1/2 tsp. cream of tartar
1/2 tsp. salt
1 tsp. baking soda
1/2 tsp. vanilla

Keep 4 qts freshly popped Orville Redenbacher's® Gourmet® Popping Corn warm in a large baking pan in oven at 200°F. In a medium saucepan, combine sugar, corn syrup, water, butter, cream of tartar, and salt. Bring to a boil, stirring constantly. Cook to 260°F on candy thermometer (hard ball stage)* without stirring. Remove from heat. *Reserve about 2 tablespoons syrup* to use in attaching decorations. Keep warm over hot water. Add baking soda and vanilla to remaining syrup; stir in quickly but thoroughly. Pour at once while foamy over warm popped corn; mix gently to coat corn. Return to oven at 200°F for 30 minutes; stir occasionally.

---

*Hard ball stage—when boiling syrup dropped into very cold water forms a hard ball.

Christmas Snowman

---

2 recipes Basic Syrup Mixture
8 quarts popped Orville Redenbacher's® Gourmet®
  Popping Corn
2 wooden skewers or dowels for arms
  gum drop candies (licorice and fruit-flavored);
    peppermint candies; toothpicks (optional);
    cloth scarf; poster paper, tape, ribbon, or
    yarn trim for hat

Prepare *1 recipe* of Basic Syrup Mixture (see page 85) with 4 quarts popped Orville Redenbacher's® Gourmet® Popping Corn, according to directions. Form into large ball for bottom of snowman. Prepare *second recipe* of popcorn mixture; form into *2 balls*, one for body of snowman and one slightly smaller for head; reserve a small amount to cover wooden skewers for arms. Stack balls together and press gently to make secure. Press reserved popcorn mixture onto two wooden skewers for arms. Insert in middle ball at "shoulders" of snowman. Makes 1 (16-inch) snowman.

Make face on snowman using gum drop candies. Add additional gum drop candies to round peppermints for buttons. Use toothpicks or reserved syrup to secure candies. Wrap a narrow piece of cloth around neck for scarf; fasten with a leaf-shape gum drop candy. Place an additional leaf-shape candy on the end of each arm for mittens. Make hat from poster paper; trim with ribbon or yarn and decorate with candies, if desired.

Snowball Candle Holders

Make ½ recipe of Basic Syrup Mixture, according to directions. Form into 3-inch balls. Place on small paper doilies, foil trays, or coasters. Insert plastic candle holder with small candle in top of each. Makes 8 to 10 candle holders.

☞ 25 ☜
Popcorn and the Pop-ettes

Popcorn and kids have a natural affinity; it's one of those synergistic things you read about.

I can remember back when I was a kid and I'd hear my mother getting the popping pan out . . . something would happen to me and I'd race through my chores or my homework or I'd get out of a blue mood if I was in one. The more I heard the popcorn pop, the happier I'd get.

Now, I know there's a school of thought that says you should never bribe children. It's bad for their characters, say the experts. If it soothes your parental principles, you can call it a reward instead. I tell you, it works wonders.

It worked that way with my daughters, and it still does with my grandkids. Popcorn is the first thing they learned to love after peanut butter sandwiches.

If you want a special bribe—I mean, reward—for a special child, or for a special occasion, try some of these recipes. My family has had first-hand experience (and first-rate success) with them. (Peanut Butter Nougat Bars happen to be one of my favorites too.)

Peanut Butter Nougat Bars

  1 (6-oz.) pkg. butterscotch pieces
  ⅓ cup peanut butter
  2 tbs. butter or margarine
  3 cups miniature marshmallows
  ¼ tsp. salt
  2½ qts. popped Orville Redenbacher's® Gourmet®
       Popping Corn
  1 cup granola
  1 (6-oz.) pkg. semi-sweet chocolate pieces

Melt butterscotch pieces, peanut butter, butter or margarine, marshmallows, and salt in top part of a double boiler over hot water. Stir constantly until melted and smooth. Combine with popped corn and granola in a buttered 9 × 13 × 2-inch pan. Toss until well mixed; press smooth in pan. Melt chocolate over hot, not boiling, water; spread over nougat mixture to form lacy pattern. Cool until firm; cut into 1 × 2-inch bars. Makes about 54 pieces.

Clowns display entry in a pop art contest sponsored by Orville.

Paddle-Pops

6 tbs. butter
3 cups miniature marshmallows
3 tbs. flavored gelatin (orange, cherry, or
   strawberry)
3 qts. popped Orville Redenbacher's® Gourmet®
   Popping Corn
12 popsicle sticks
1 bottle of your favorite cake decorator sprinkles

In a medium saucepan, melt butter and miniature marshmallows over low heat; stir in flavored gelatin. Pour over popcorn in a large bowl; mix gently to coat corn.

With buttered hands, scoop out about a cupful and shape around a popsicle stick. Make any shape you wish (a ball, oblong, square, etc). Sprinkle with cake sprinkles. Repeat for each stick. Makes 8 pops.

Here are some more of my favorites. They're definitely kid-pleasers, but I love 'em too because I'm still young at heart.

Paddle-Pops

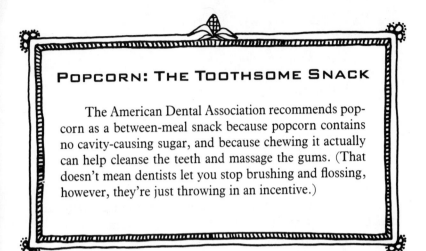

POPCORN: THE TOOTHSOME SNACK

The American Dental Association recommends popcorn as a between-meal snack because popcorn contains no cavity-causing sugar, and because chewing it actually can help cleanse the teeth and massage the gums. (That doesn't mean dentists let you stop brushing and flossing, however, they're just throwing in an incentive.)

Blockbuster Crunch

4 qts. popped Orville Redenbacher's® Gourmet® Popping Corn
½ cup raisins
½ cup chopped dried apricots
½ cup salted cocktail peanuts
¼ cup hulled sunflower seeds
6 caramel sheets for wrapping apples

Combine popped corn, raisins, apricots, peanuts, and seeds. Put half of popcorn mixture into each of two shallow baking pans, buttered. Unwrap 6 caramel sheets. Stretch caramel sheets very thin. Lay 3 sheets over the popcorn in each pan. Bake the popcorn at 250° F for 15–20 minutes, until caramel melts. Carefully remove popcorn from the oven and pour back into the large bowl. Stir with a long wooden spoon until the popcorn is well coated with caramel. Lay two long pieces of wax paper on the counter or table; spread popcorn on them. Let stand until cool. Makes 4 quarts.

Marshmallow Munch Balls

1 (7-oz.) jar marshmallow cream
¾ cup peanut butter
2 tbs. milk
2 qts. popped Orville Redenbacher's® Gourmet®
    Popping Corn
½ cup salted cocktail peanuts
25 milk chocolate candy kisses

In a large bowl, combine marshmallow cream, peanut butter, and milk. Stir until creamy. Add popped corn and cocktail peanuts. Mix until coated. Grease hands well with butter. Form popcorn mixture into 2-inch balls. Place on butter cookie sheets. Press one milk chocolate candy kiss into the top of each ball. Bake at 375° F for 5 minutes. Let balls cool on cookie sheets for 20 minutes. Makes 25 2-inch popcorn balls.

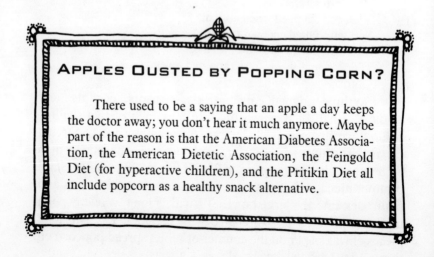

APPLES OUSTED BY POPPING CORN?

There used to be a saying that an apple a day keeps the doctor away; you don't hear it much anymore. Maybe part of the reason is that the American Diabetes Association, the American Dietetic Association, the Feingold Diet (for hyperactive children), and the Pritikin Diet all include popcorn as a healthy snack alternative.

Crunchy Popcorn Freeze

2 tbs. butter or margarine
1/4 cup dark brown sugar
2 cups popped Orville Redenbacher's® Gourmet®
    Popping Corn
1/3 cup crushed peanut brittle
1 qt. vanilla ice cream, softened

Melt butter or margarine in a skillet. Add sugar; heat and stir over low heat until blended. Add popcorn and peanut brittle; toss to coat well. Cool; break into chunks. Stir ice cream and fold in 1½ cups popcorn chunks. Spoon into 8 paper cupcake liners. Freeze until firm. Sprinkle with remaining popcorn before serving. Makes 8 servings.

Sunny Lemon Popcorn Balls

1 cup light corn syrup
1 tsp. white vinegar
2 tbs. butter or margarine
1/2 tsp. lemon extract
5 drops yellow food coloring
2 qts. popped Orville Redenbacher's® Gourmet®
    Popping Corn
1/2 cup crushed lemon drop candies

Combine corn syrup and vinegar in saucepan; boil slowly until syrup reaches 260°F on candy thermometer (hard ball stage).* Remove from heat and stir in butter or margarine, lemon extract, and food coloring. Combine popcorn and lemon drops in a large lightly buttered bowl; pour syrup over. Toss until evenly coated. With lightly buttered hands, shape mixture into 2½ inch balls and place on buttered plate. Makes 1 dozen balls.

---

*Hard ball stage—when boiling syrup dropped into very cold water forms a hard ball.

☞ 26 ☜
Belly to Belly, Ear to Ear, and People to People

I've done a good deal of traveling in my day, and my day is far from over. So far, I've visited ninety-six different countries, some just for vacationing purposes, but many of them as one of the Good-Will Ambassadors serving with the government-sponsored People to People to Program.

Some of my favorite spots were those countries to which we had been shipping popcorn seed—you could say I had a vested interest in them: Israel (where I was awarded a special citation for helping save their popcorn crop—one of the important cash crops of that nation's economy), Greece, Hungary, Yugoslavia, France, Italy, South Africa, Colombia, and Argentina (where popcorn is extremely popular; there are popcorn vendors on street corners everywhere).

Climatically speaking, and as regards soil conditions, I've always felt that the east-central part of China would be perfect for popcorn crops. But farmland is valuable there, so they're going to wait until we develop a higher-yield popcorn seed before they try it.

Of course, you know that we Americans love popcorn. In fact, for the past seven years, Orville Redenbacher's® Gourmet® Popping Corn has been the official popcorn of Disneyland and Disneyworld. But for those of you who seek a foreign flair, here are some 'Round the World recipes to whet your appetite.

Mexicali Corn Bowl

- ⅓ cup butter or margarine
- 1 tbs. dry taco seasoning mix
- 1 tbs. dry chopped chives
- 4 qts. popped Orville Redenbacher's® Gourmet® Popping Corn

In a small saucepan, melt butter or margarine over low heat. Add taco seasoning mix and chives. Blend well. Pour seasoned butter mixture over popcorn in a large serving bowl and toss lightly but thoroughly. Serve at once. Makes 4 quarts.

Mexicali Corn Bowl

Chinese Popcorn

- 1 (3-oz.) can Chinese chow mein noodles
- 2 tbs. sesame seeds
- 2 tsp. dried chives
- ½ tsp. garlic salt
- ¼ tsp. ground ginger
- 2 qts. popped Orville Redenbacher's® Gourmet® Popping Corn

Combine dried ingredients. Pour over freshly popped corn. Toss gently. Makes 2 quarts.

Teriyaki Corn Bowl

Teriyaki Corn Bowl

- 2 tsp. soy sauce
- 1 tsp. ground ginger
- ½ tsp. onion salt
- ⅓ cup butter or margarine
- 3 tbs. pure Wesson® Oil or Orville Redenbacher's® Gourmet® Buttery Flavor® Popping Oil
- ½ cup Orville Redenbacher's® Gourmet® Popping Corn

In a small saucepan, blend soy sauce, ginger, and onion salt until well mixed. Add butter or margarine and melt over low heat. Keep mixture warm while preparing popcorn. Measure oil and popcorn into 4-qt. popper or pan; place, covered, over medium high heat or follow manufacturer's directions for electric popper. When popping slows, remove from heat and allow popping to continue on stored heat. Empty into a large serving bowl. Stir seasoned mixture, pour over popcorn, and toss lightly but thoroughly. Serve at once. Makes 4 quarts.

Italienne Corn Bowl

⅓ cup butter or margarine
1 tsp. Italian herb seasoning
1 tsp. minced parsley
½ tsp. garlic salt
2–3 tbs. grated Parmesean cheese
3 tbs. pure Wesson® Oil or Orville Redenbacher's® Gourmet® Buttery Flavor® Popping Oil
½ cup unpopped Orville Redenbacher's® Gourmet® Popping Corn

Melt butter in a small saucepan over low heat. Add herb seasoning, parsley, garlic salt, and cheese; blend well. Keep mixture warm while preparing popcorn. Empty popcorn into a large serving bowl. Stir seasoned butter mixture, pour over popcorn, and toss lightly but thoroughly. Serve at once. Makes 4 quarts.

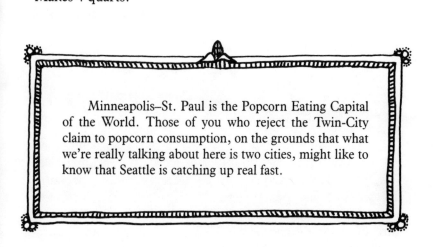

Minneapolis–St. Paul is the Popcorn Eating Capital of the World. Those of you who reject the Twin-City claim to popcorn consumption, on the grounds that what we're really talking about here is two cities, might like to know that Seattle is catching up real fast.

☞ Afterword ☜
Instituting Order in the Popcorn Field

As you know, I've been in the popcorn field virtually all my life. Over thirty years ago, I was involved with a number of other popcorn professionals in forming The Popcorn Institute, an association of processors and others concerned with the propagation, promotion, and potential of the popping corn business.

Through The Popcorn Institute, we've accomplished a great deal. We've gone a long way toward weeding out the chaff in the field, for instance, and improving popping corn. We've instituted the Seal of Quality Performance for popcorn poppers that meet our rigid standards. We've gathered information on the history of popcorn and on its nutritional merits. We've pooled our knowledge for the betterment of the industry. And we've had a lot of fun promoting popping corn both here and abroad.

We've even gotten the entire month of October, including Halloween, of course, officially designated each year as National Popcorn Month. (You be sure to celebrate, you hear?) And Valparaiso, Indiana, dedicates a week of festivities to honor popcorn. Their Annual Popcorn Festival, held in September, is not to be missed!

I want, here and now, to thank The Popcorn Institute and my fellow members for their help in all we've achieved. Especially, I thank them for teaching me how to spell the Indian name "Quadequina."